HOW TO TIE FLIES

The Barnes Sports Library

This library of practical sports books covers fundamentals, techniques, coaching and playing hints and equipment for each sport. Leading coaches and players have been selected to write these books, so each volume is authoritative and based upon actual experience. Photographs or drawings, or both, illustrate techniques, equipment and play.

ARCHERY
  by Reichart & Keasey
BAIT CASTING
  by Gilmer Robinson
BASEBALL
  by Daniel E. Jessee
BASKETBALL
  by Charles C. Murphy
BASKETBALL FOR GIRLS
  by Meissner & Meyers
BASKETBALL OFFICIATING
  by Dave Tobey
BETTER BADMINTON
  by Jackson & Swan
BICYCLING
  by Ruth & Raymond Benedict
BOWLING
  by Falcaro & Goodman
BOXING
  by Edwin L. Haislet
CHEERLEADING
  by Loken & Dypwick
FENCING
  by Joseph Vince
FIELD HOCKEY FOR GIRLS
  by Josephine T. Lees
FLY CASTING
  by Gilmer Robinson
FOOTBALL
  by W. Glenn Killinger
FUNDAMENTAL HANDBALL
  by Bernath E. Phillips
GOLF
  by Patty Berg
HANDBALL
  by Bernath E. Phillips
HOW TO TIE FLIES
  by E. C. Cregg
ICE HOCKEY
  by Edward Jeremiah
JIU-JITSU
  by Frederick P. Lowell
LACROSSE
  by Tad Stanwick

LAWN GAMES
  by John R. Tunis
PADDLE TENNIS
  by Fessenden S. Blanchard
PHYSICAL CONDITIONING
  by Stafford & Duncan
RIDING
  by J. J. Boniface
RIFLE MARKSMANSHIP
  by Lt. Wm. L. Stephens
ROLLER SKATING
  by Bob Martin
ROPING
  by Bernard S. Mason
SIX-MAN FOOTBALL
  by Ray O. Duncan
SKATING
  by Putnam & Parkinson
SKIING
  by Walter Prager
SOCCER AND SPEEDBALL
FOR GIRLS
  by Florence L. Hupprich
SOCCER
  by Samuel Fralick
SOFTBALL
  by Arthur T. Noren
SWIMMING
  by R. J. H. Kiphuth
TABLE TENNIS
  by Jay Purves
TENNIS
  by Helen Jacobs
TENNIS MADE EASY
  by Lloyd Budge
TOUCH FOOTBALL
  by John V. Grombach
TRACK AND FIELD
  by Ray M. Conger
VOLLEY BALL
  by Robert Laveaga
WRESTLING
  by E. C. Gallagher

Clair Bee's Basketball Library

THE SCIENCE OF COACHING :: MAN-TO-MAN DEFENSE AND ATTACK
ZONE DEFENSE AND ATTACK :: DRILLS AND FUNDAMENTALS

HOW TO TIE FLIES

BY

E. C. GREGG

DRAWINGS AND PHOTOGRAPHS
BY THE AUTHOR

A. S. BARNES AND COMPANY

NEW YORK

CONTENTS

INTRODUCTION   vii

TOOLS, HOOKS AND MATERIALS   1
    Tools—Fly-Tier's Vise, Hackle Pliers, Scissors
    Hooks
    Materials—Quill Bodies, Herl Bodies, Hackles,
        Tails, Cheeks or Shoulders, Ribbing,
        Wings, Wax, Tying Silk

BUCKTAIL STREAMERS   15

WET FLIES   22

DRY FLIES   27

NYMPHS and Their Construction   32
    Nymphs: Their Construction
    The Helgramite

BASS FLIES AND FEATHER STREAMERS   42

FAMOUS BUCKTAIL AND FEATHER STREAMERS   47

FLOATING BUGS and Their Construction   49
    Cork Bodied Bass Bugs

ANGLERS' KNOTS   61

MY FAVORITE FLIES   62

STANDARD DRESSINGS OF 334 FLIES   69

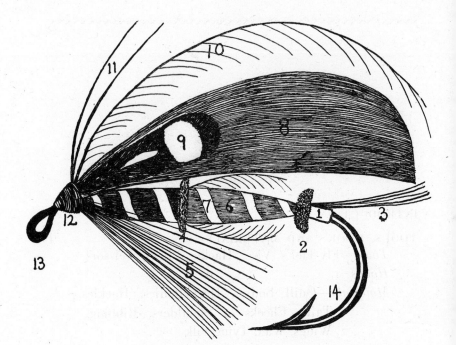

PARTS OF A FLY

1 The Tag	8 Wing
2 The Butt	9 Cheek
3 The Tail	10 Topping
4 Joint	11 Horns
5 Hackle	12 Head
6 Body	13 Eye
7 Ribbing	14 Hook

DIAGRAM 1

◇◇◇

INTRODUCTION

THE OBJECT OF THIS BOOK will be throughout its entirety to teach in a practical manner the Art of Fly Tying in all its branches. The principles used herein, and the methods of construction employed, are those used by the professional fly-tier who practices fly-making for the sake of art, and tries to achieve with each finished fly, a masterpiece.

None of the short-cuts employed by those whose business is quantity production will be attempted. Only the making of flies of the very highest quality and most durable construction will be attempted. In describing the principles of construction with the following illustrations, it will be impossible to describe in detail each standard pattern; however, it must be remembered that the fundamentals applying to each style of fly will be the principal basis of construction of all flies of that style, and that the use of different body materials, hackles, wings or size will simply change the pattern and not the fundamental points of construction.

Dressings for hundreds of standard patterns will be found fully described elsewhere in this book. For clearness of understanding please note that where a fly is described in this book as having grey wings, or red body, etc., and no particular feather or material is specified, it means that any feather or body material may be used. When a particular feather, body, hackle, tail, etc., must be used it will be so stated.

Each year a steadily increasing number of anglers are learning to tie their own flies. Not many years ago, there were few in America outside of professional tiers, who understood the art. Now on each angling trip, at least one is sure to be met, who has discovered the great thrill of taking fish on flies of his own tying.

To those who are anticipating the making of their own flies for the first time, there is the opportunity to exercise one's ingenuity in the creation of new patterns. To prolong your fishing seasons throughout the long winter evenings, in the confines of your own den, where, with a supply of fur, feathers and tinsel, can be enjoyed a profitable, artistic and pleasant hobby. And the thrill of seeing in each finished imitation of Ephemeridae, Muscidae and Formicidae, a masterpiece to bring the joy of living and dreams of spring to the angler's heart.

Beginners are requested to reject any inclination to skip over the first part of this book, nor to attempt the tying of the more delicate and difficult dry flies before they have had sufficient preliminary training.

This book is so written that the easier flies to make are the first encountered. Although you may not expect to use Bucktail Streamers, the fundamental principles employed in their construction, the knack of handling fur, feathers and tinsel, will be acquired, and a sense of proportion will be realized. I sincerely encourage you to begin at the beginning, and by careful and patient study the satisfactory result will be the ability to make flies that are second to none.

The illustrations in this book are all drawn to correct proportions except the tying silk, which is purposely drawn large for clearness of illustration. Follow these illustrations, and begin by making a very careful study of Diagram 3, "Bucktails" (page 16). Here will be learned how to overcome some of the difficulties encountered by beginners. Many of the fundamentals learned in tying Bucktails are used in tying all of the flies to follow. For instance, in putting the wings or tail on a wet fly, the same method of holding the wing between the thumb and finger, and making the loose loop, are explained as when putting the hair or tail on a Bucktail. Putting the wings on a fly correctly seems to be the greatest difficulty encountered by the beginner. Consequently, the necessity of carefully studying Figs. 4, 5, 10, and 11 of Diagram 3 cannot be too greatly emphasized. Before tying any other part of the fly, place a bare hook in the vise, and practice tying on the tail, and then the wings, until you have mastered this knack, and have the wings and tail setting straight on top of the hook, as in Figs. 4, 5, 10 and 11 of Diagram 3. First using hair and then a section of feather.

Other faults of the beginner where literal descriptions are followed entirely, or where illustrations are not drawn to correct proportions or followed closely, are as follows. The wings are usually too large, and much too long for the size of the hook, and the tail is most always too long, as are the hackles. The bodies seldom have a nicely tapered shape, and most always start too far back on the hook shank. The ribbing is seldom put on in even tight spirals. The hair on hair flies is always too long, and too much is used. The head is too large, because the tying silk is not wound tightly and smoothly. The eye of the hook on the finished fly is filled with hair, tying silk, hackles and cement.

I do not mean to criticize these common mistakes of the beginner. Instead, I merely wish to call them to your mind, and assure you that they are not necessary, and will not happen if you will diligently follow instructions in this book.

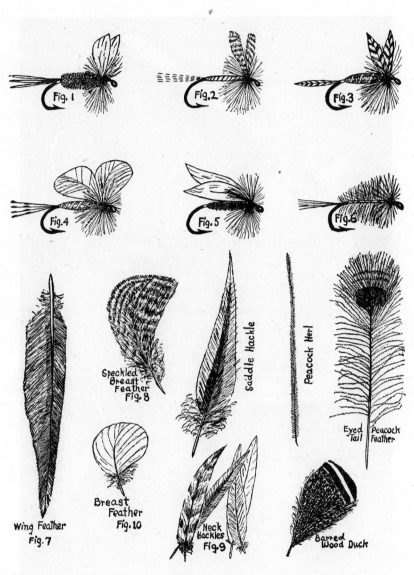

Fig. 1

Fig. 2

Fig. 3

Fig. 4

Fig. 5

Fig. 6

Speckled Breast Feather Fig. 8

Saddle Hackle

Peacock Herl

Wing Feather Fig. 7

Breast Feather Fig. 10

Neck Hackles Fig. 9

Eyed Tail

Peacock Feather

Barred Wood Duck

DIAGRAM 2

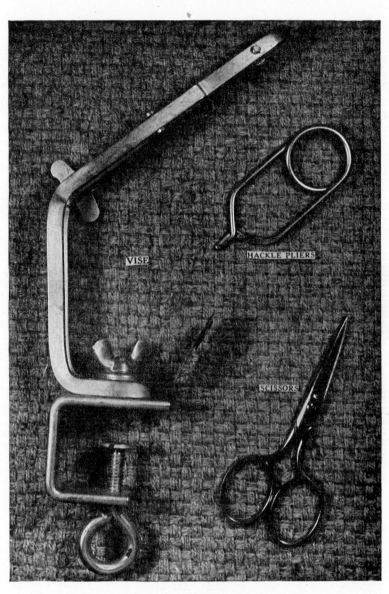

Tools two-thirds actual size

TOOLS, HOOKS AND
MATERIALS

Very few tools are required by the Fly-Tier. Those that are necessary are inexpensive, and most of them can be homemade. However, as with any other craft, good tools are an asset. I advise the beginner to procure the following:

TOOLS

Fly-Tiers' vise. There are many styles of fly-tying vises on the market. The simplest is just a slot cut in a $\frac{3}{8}''$ piece of square steel with a hacksaw, and a thumb screw to tighten the slot. This type of vise will work all right, although rather clumsy and hard to tighten enough to hold the hook firmly. Another simple vise is just a small pin chuck, soldered to one end of a $\frac{1}{4}''$ brass rod, bent at the desired angle, and the other end of the rod soldered to a small G clamp. However, I prefer a vise of the cam lever type. That is, a vise that has a cam lever for opening and closing the jaws. These vises, of which there are several makes, are

1

adjustable to various angles and hook sizes. They will hold all sizes of hooks very firmly, and are easily and quickly opened or closed with just a flip of the lever.

Hackle Pliers. These can be purchased for about fifty cents and will prove a worthwhile investment, as they are rather difficult to make satisfactorily.

Scissors. One pair with curved blades and sharp points for small flies, and one pair with small straight blades. A needle pushed into a stick, for picking out hackles that are wound under, and for putting lacquer on the finished head, completes the list of necessary tools.

HOOKS

Hooks used for fly-tying differ somewhat from those used for bait fishing, etc., inasmuch as they are usually hollow ground, and tapered shank, especially those used for dry flies. The tapered shank next to the eye allows the head of the fly to be tied smaller, and also reduces the weight of the hook, an advantage for dry flies. Of course flies may be tied on any style or grade of hook, but considering the work involved in making the fly, and realizing that with an old razor blade the fly can be quickly removed from the hook should the first attempts prove unsatisfactory, you will see the advantage in using good hooks.

2

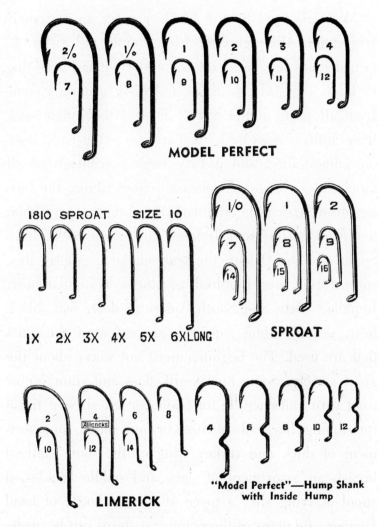

MODEL PERFECT

1810 SPROAT   SIZE 10

1X 2X 3X 4X 5X 6XLONG

SPROAT

LIMERICK

"Model Perfect"—Hump Shank
with Inside Hump

Various styles of hooks used for fly-tying—actual size

MATERIALS

Materials used by the Fly-Tier cover an extremely large field. Although only a few simple and easily obtained items are necessary for a start, it is interesting to know that furs, feathers and body materials come from all parts of the world. There's the jungle cock from India whose neck feathers are extensively used on salmon flies, and a very large percentage of all fancy flies. The golden pheasant from China, the bustard from Africa, the Mandarin wood duck from China, the capercailzie from Ireland, the game cocks from Spain and the Orient, the teal, mallard, grouse, ibis, swan, turkey, and hundreds of others. The polar bear, Impalla, North and South American deer, seal, black bear, skunk, rabbit, squirrel, are a few of the hairs that are used. The beginner need not worry about the great variety. Some hooks, silk floss and spun fur or wool yarn and chenille for bodies, a few sizes of tinsel for ribbing, bucktails of three or four colors, an assortment of duck and turkey wing quills, some mallard breast, an assortment of neck and saddle hackles, a spool of tying silk, a piece of wax, a bottle of head lacquer, and many of the popular patterns can be made. Numerous other items can be added from time to time, and the novice Fly-Tier will soon find himself in possession of a collection of fuzzy furs and feathers that

4

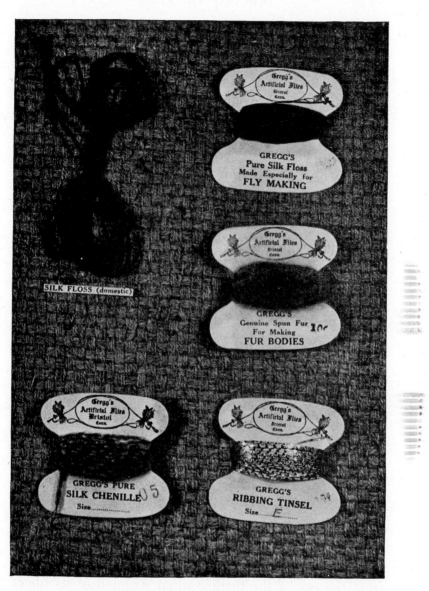

Body materials two-thirds actual size

will delight the heart of any professional, and from which any conceivable lure can be made to attract the denizens of the shady pools.

BODY MATERIAL: Tinsel, Silk Floss, Fur, Chenille, Wool, Quill and Cork are used for bodies. The most commonly used for Bucktail Streamers is flat tinsel ribbed with an oval tinsel or no ribbing at all. About the easiest body to make is one of chenille ribbed with tinsel. Silk floss is mostly used for wet and dry fly bodies. The domestic silk floss, which is called rope, can be successfully used for the larger flies, by untwisting and using a few of the smaller strands. An imported floss of one single strand, with a very slight twist, is especially made for fly-tying; this will work much better on the smaller hooks. Fur for fur bodies, which formerly had to be plucked from the hide, dyed the desired color, and spun on the waxed tying silk, can now be obtained in all standard fly colors. It is called Spun Fur, and is very convenient to use in this manner.

QUILL BODIES: Quill makes an excellent and very lifelike body, especially on dry flies. The quill from the eyed peacock tail feather is mostly used. That taken from the eye of the feather when stripped of its fibers has a two tone effect, and when wound upon the hook without overlapping makes a very lifelike and delicate appearing body.

Actual size

HERL BODIES: Both peacock and ostrich herl is used for bodies. These make a fuzzy body. Tie in one or two strands by the tip end and wind on edgewise.

HACKLES: These are the most important part of the dry fly. Only those from the neck of a mature cock are satisfactory. Hackles for the dry fly must be stiff with very little or no web. With such hackles a dry fly can be sparsely dressed as it should be and still mainatin its natural balance and floating qualities. On the other hand, a wet fly should sink readily, and should be made with very soft webby hackles. These absorb water quickly, and have better action in the water. Contrary to the customary way to tie hackles on the wet fly, as explained in the chapter "Wet Flies," I find it very convenient and economical to strip the fibers from any size hackle, clip off the butt ends to the desired length and tie them on the bottom of the hook, the same as bucktail is tied on. As wet flies should have hackles only on the bottom or underneath side, many hackles that are otherwise too large can be used in this way.

TAILS: A few fibers from a golden or silver pheasant neck tippet, whisks from a hackle feather, a strip of wing or breast feather, a few hairs, etc., are used for tails. Many of the standard patterns are tied without tails; however, on all of my dry flies, I tie three or four stiff fibers or hairs. They balance the fly and help it to float much better.

8

Two-thirds actual size

CHEEKS OR SHOULDERS: As per Fig. 9, Diagram 1, these are used on a great many of the fancy flies. These are strips of one or several feathers of contrasting colors. Jungle cock feathers, golden pheasant tippets, silver pheasant body feathers, as on the Grey Ghost streamer fly, blue chatterer, and many other fancy feathers according to pattern and fancy are used for this purpose. A pair of jungle cock tippets, often called eyes, added to a Bucktail Streamer will often take trout, when the same pattern without the jungle cock will not.

RIBBING: Tinsel, Wool, Silk, Horse Hair, Quill, etc., are used for ribbing. The tinsel from your Xmas tree will do, but it is much better to use tinsel made for the purpose, as it will not tarnish so quickly and is much stronger. It is advisable before using tinsel to place a drop of good, clear head lacquer between the thumb and finger and draw the tinsel through it. This makes it tarnish-proof, and is particularly advisable with the oval and round tinsel that is wound over a silk core. Besides tarnish-proofing it, it will keep the tinsel from coming apart. Tinsel bodies should be lacquered after they are finished.

WINGS: Several styles of wings are used, see Diagram 2, page xi, those on Fig. 1, and are cut from a pair of matched wing quill feathers, like Fig. 7. Those in Fig. 2 are buzz wings taken from a pair of breast feathers

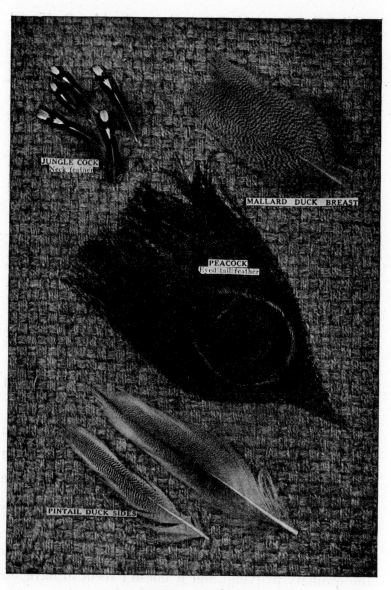

Two-thirds actual size

(mallard, wood duck, etc.) shown in Fig. 8. Fig. 3 shows hackle tip wings, tips of two hackle feathers, see Fig. 9. Fan wings, Fig. 4, are a matched pair of small breastfeathers, see Fig. 10 (white duck, mallard, teal, grouse, etc.). In fact there is hardly a bird that flies that does not supply some of its plumage to the Fly-Tier. Flies of the order Diptera (land flies), such as the Bee, Cowdung, Blue Bottle, etc., should be tied with flat wings as in Fig. 5. A Bi-visible is shown in Fig. 6. This is a fly without wings, hackle tied palmer (that is hackle wound the full length of the hook, usually tied without a body, and the dark patterns have a turn or two of white hackle in front).

All of the flies on Diagram 2 are shown as dry flies; however, the same feathers are used for wet flies, streamers, etc., the difference being the style in which they are tied, which is explained elsewhere.

WAX: Use a good grade of wax for fly-tying. The proper wax will work much better than shoemaker's wax or beeswax. Wax for fly-tying should be quite sticky so that when the waxed tying silk is let go of, it will not unwind while tying the fly.

TYING SILK: Ordinary sewing silk is too coarse for the ordinary fly-tying, and it doesn't seem to have the strength. Size 00 is a good size for all flies, including bucktails and streamers. For dry flies and small wet flies a gossamer silk size 000 and 0000 is the best to

Two-thirds actual size

use. Although the strength of this fine silk is much less than the size 00, it has the advantage that more turns can be used, and the heads can be made much smaller.

BUCKTAIL STREAMERS

PLACE A HOOK in the vise and start waxed tying silk (See Diagram 3, page 16) (A) ⅛″ from eye of hook Fig. 1. Take five or six turns and cut off end (B) Fig. 2. Wind tying silk (A) closely and smoothly down hook shank as Fig. 3. (A complete understanding of the next step will have a great deal to do with the success of the beginner's greatest difficulty, that is, putting on the wings; the procedure is the same for all flies, study Fig. 4.) Hold tail material (C) between thumb and finger of the left hand, slide the fingers down over the hook, so that the tail material rests on top of the hook, with the hook held firmly between thumb and finger as Fig. 4. Now loosen grip just enough to allow tying silk (A) to pass up between thumb and tail material, form · a loose loop over material, and down, between finger and material on the other side. Now tighten grip with thumb and finger and pull loop down tight, repeat once more, see Fig. 5. (This knack of holding the material and hook firmly together, until the loose loop is drawn down tightly keeps the tail, or wings, on top of the

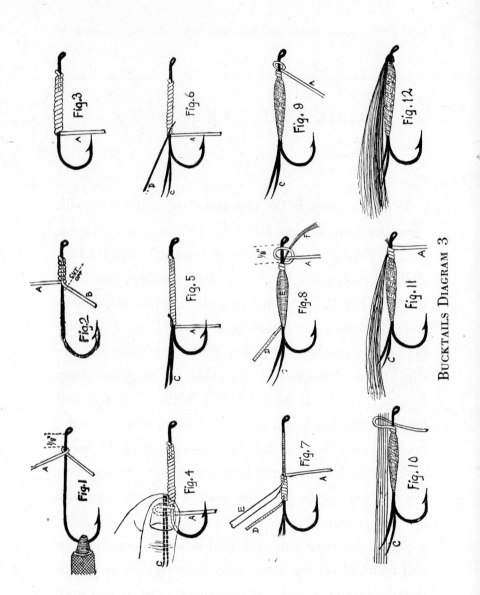

BUCKTAILS DIAGRAM 3

hook, and at the same time keeps them from splitting or turning sidewise.) Now that the tail is in place, with two turns of the tying silk (A) tie in ribbing (D) Fig. 6. Now take six or eight close tight turns with the tying silk towards the eye of the hook, with two more turns tie in the body material (E) Fig. 7. IF USING TINSEL FOR BODY MATERIAL, BE SURE AND CUT THE END TO A TAPER BEFORE TYING IN as (E) Fig. 7; this tends to make a smoother body and prevents a bunch where the body material is tied in. Next wind tying silk (A) back to the starting point, take a half hitch and let it hang. Now wind body material (E) clockwise (all windings are clockwise) tightly and smoothly back towards the barb, to the extreme rear end of the body, pull tight and wind forward to within $\frac{1}{8}''$ of the eye, wind back and forth to form smooth tapered body as Fig. 8 (tinsel bodies are not tapered). (If using silk floss, untwist the floss and use only one half or one third of the strands, do not let it twist, wind tight, and it will make a nice smooth body.) Take two turns and a half hitch with the tying silk, and cut off end of the material (F) Fig. 8. Take one tight turn with ribbing

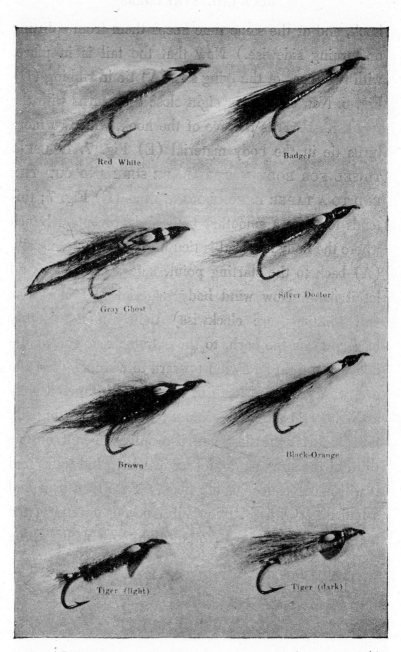

Bucktail streamers tied by the author (actual size)

Two-thirds actual size

(D) over butt of tail close to rear end of the body, also one turn under the tail if tail is to be cocked. Wind ribbing spirally around the body and tie off with two turns and a half hitch of tying silk as Fig. 9.

Take about three dozen hairs of colored bucktail, cut off butt ends to the length wanted for the finished fly, not more than one half again as long as the hook, place these on top of the hook as Fig. 10 with butt ends about 1-16″ back of the eye (this is held the same as when putting on the tail, Fig. 4). Pull down two or three loops, Fig. 11. Now take about 175 hairs of other colored bucktail, place this on top of the first colored bucktail the same as Fig. 10. Repeat the same operation as Fig. 11. Before finishing the head put a drop of head lacquer on the butt ends of the hairs to cement them in place, finish by making a smooth tapered head with the tying silk, take three or four half hitches, paint the head with two or three coats of lacquer and the job is complete, unless you wish to add jungle cock cheeks, or other combinations of feathers. This of course is done before the head is completed.

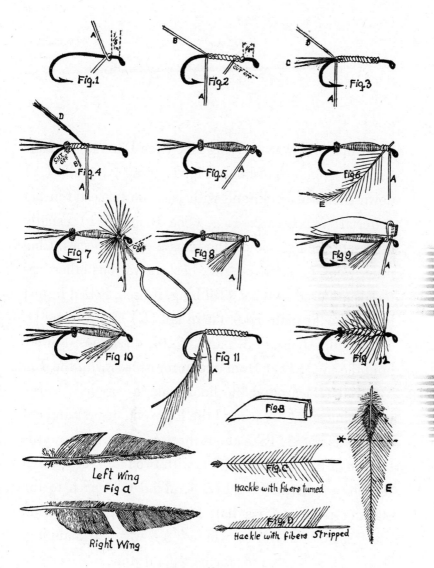

Fig.1 Fig.2 Fig.3 Fig.4 Fig.5 Fig.6

Fig.7 Fig.8 Fig.9 Fig.10 Fig.11 Fig.12

Fig.B

Fig.C
Hackle with fibers turned

Fig.D
Hackle with fibers Stripped

Left Wing
Fig a

Right Wing

DIAGRAM 4

WET FLIES

START THE WAXED tying silk (See Diagram 4, page 21) ⅛" from eye of hook, Fig. 1. Wind tying silk (A) down shank of hook, and with last two turns tie in tag material (B) Fig. 2. Tags (See Diagram 1) usually represent the egg sac on the female of the species. Chenille, wool, gold, silver, silk, herl, or various other materials are used for tags. (Ribbing, if used, is tied in just before the tag material.) Tie in tail (C) Fig. 3 (see Fig. 4 Bucktail, Diagram 3, page 16, for directions, how to hold the tail). Take from one to four turns with the Tag Material (B) around the hook, take a couple of turns with tying silk (A) around the loose end of (B) and cut off (B) as Fig. 4. Take about three or four turns towards the eye of the hook with (A), with two more turns tie in the body material (D) Fig. 4. Wind (A) back to the starting point, take a half hitch and let hang. Wind body material (D) to where (A) was left hanging. Wind (D) back and forth several times to form a tapered body, fasten with two or three turns and a half hitch with (A) Fig. 5. Next take hackle (E), and strip off soft web fibers on dotted line, Fig. E. Hold hackle

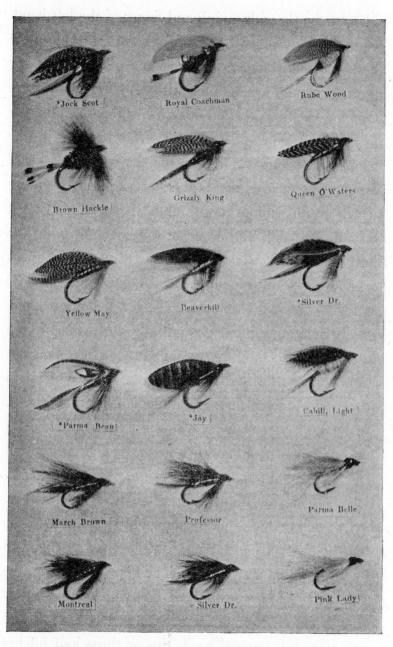

Wet flies tied by the author (actual size)

(E) by the tip with thumb and finger of the left hand, with the shiny side of the hackle to the right, place the butt diagonally under the hook and take four or five tight turns and a half hitch with (A) Fig. 6. Be sure that the hackle is tied on edgewise with the shiny side to the front. Now grasp the tip of the hackle with the hackle pliers and wind four or five turns clockwise around the hook. If the hackle starts winding edgewise it will go on without any trouble, if not better take it off and try again until you get the knack of tying the butt in at just the right angle. Take three or four turns over the hackle tip with (A) and clip off the tip close as Fig. 7. With the thumb and finger of the left hand, reach from under the hook and pull all the fibers down to the bottom, take three or four turns over them with (A) towards the barb of the hook, to hold them in place, and to keep them pointing well back, as Fig. 8. Next take a pair of matched (one right and one left) turkey, goose, or other wing feathers, Fig. A, and cut a section from each about ¼" wide, place the two sections with tips even and concave sides together as Fig. B. Cut off the butt ends to the right length, that is so that the tips come even, or a little beyond the bend of the hook. Place on top of hook as Fig. 9 and tie on the same as previously explained in tying hair on Bucktails (Diagram 3, page 16, Figs. 4 and 10). Finish off with a smooth tapered head, two or three half hitches

WHITE TIPPED MALLARD

MALLARD DUCK WING QUILLS

BLACK TIPPED MALLARD

Two-thirds actual size

and a couple of coats of good head lacquer, Fig. 10. Many patterns are tied palmer, that is the hackle is wound the whole length of the body. Many of the dry flies are tied this way, especially the Bi-visibles. To tie a palmer hackle, prepare the hackle by holding the tip of the hackle between the thumb and finger of the left hand, and with the thumb and finger of the right hand, stroke the fibers back so that they point towards the butt, instead of towards the tip, Fig. C, Diagram 4. With the shiny side of the hackle up, strip off the fibers from the bottom side as Fig. D. Now tie the hackle in by the tip as Fig. 11. Make the body the same as before. Wind the hackle spirally around the body and tie off the butt, Fig. 12. To make the hackle more full near the head, one or more hackles are tied in at the same time, as Figs. 6 and 7, the palmer hackle is wound to within ⅛″ of the eye and the butt tied in and cut off the same as the tip was cut off, Fig. 7.

DRY FLIES

START WINDING waxed tying silk (See Diagram 5, page 28) (A) about ⅛″ from the eye of the hook, take three or four turns towards the bend of the hook and cut off end, Fig. 1, Diagram 5. Cut a section about ¼″ wide from a right and one from a left wing feather, as Fig. A, Diagram 4, page 21 (duck wings are best for dry flies). Place convex sides together (just the reverse of Fig. B, Diagram 4). Do not cut off the butt ends, instead straddle the hook as Fig. 2, Diagram 5. Hold between the thumb and finger of the left hand as already explained in Figs. 4 and 10, Diagram 3, page 16. Tip the wings (B) forward so that they stand about perpendicular to the shank, and pull down loop, Fig. 3, as explained in Diagram 3, Fig. 4. Take one more turn with (A) around the wings (B) in front as Fig. 4 and before loosening the grip with the left hand take two turns around the hook close in back of the wings (B), Fig. 5. Next pull the butt ends back tightly as Fig. 6, take two tight turns around them with (A) and cut off on dotted line as Fig. 6. Cross (A) between wings (B) to spread them, and wind tying silk (A) down shank of the hook as Fig. 7.

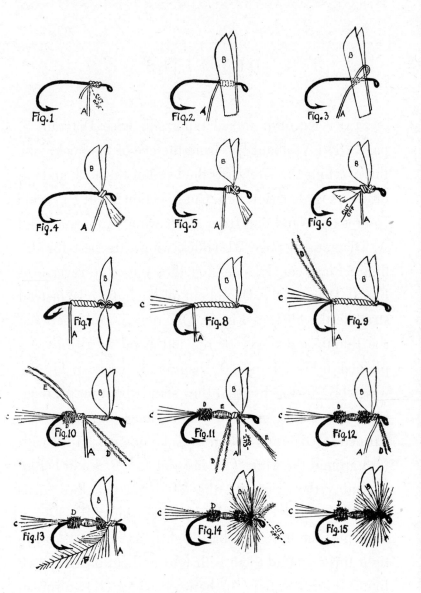

DIAGRAM 5

From now on the body is made as previously explained, so for the sake of variation we will tie a band in the centre, the same as a Royal Coachman. Tie in tail (C) Fig. 8. Tie in two or three strands of peacock herl (D) Fig. 9 with (A) and wind (A) four or five turns towards the eye of the hook. Take three or four turns with herl (D). Tie in two strands of silk floss (E) Fig. 10, take a few more turns with (A) over the loose ends of (D) towards the eye of the hook. Wind silk floss (E) over the herl about half way up the hook. Take a turn or two around silk floss (E) with (A) and cut off end of (E) as Fig. 11. Carry (A) up to the front of the wings. Finish body with herl (D) wound tight against the back of the wings. (This helps to push the wings forward and to hold them in place.) Tie off herl (D) with (A) Fig. 12. The next step of putting on the hackle (F) is done the same as Fig. 6, Diagram 4, page 21. But here the hackle is much more important than on the wet fly. The floating qualities of a dry fly depend entirely upon stiff neck hackle of the proper size. (Use Hackle Chart.) Sometimes two hackles are used, these are laid together, and both butts tied in at the same time. One hackle of the proper size and stiffness is usually enough, so we will use one tied in as Fig. 13 and explained in Fig. 6, Diagram 4, page 21. Clip the hackle pliers to the tip of hackle (F) and wind about two turns edgewise in front of the wings, wind two turns close

29

Fan Wings, Dry Flies and Nymphs tied by the author
(actual size)

in back of the wings. Take two or three more turns in front of the wings, all the while keeping the hackle edgewise, with the shiny side towards the eye of the hook. Wind the hackle close so as not to fill up the eye of the hook, and to leave room for the head. Tie in the tip with a couple of turns of (A) Fig. 14. The hackle should now be standing straight out from the hook, with the most of it in front of the wings. Shape a tapered head with (A). (Head should be about 1-16″ long on a size 12 hook.) Finish with two or three half hitches and a drop of head lacquer, Fig. 15.

Various feathers are used for wings of dry flies, such as breast feathers from mallard, teal, partridge, grouse, black duck, wood duck. Hackle tips, starling, duck, turkey, goose, pheasant, wing feathers, etc.

Two whole feathers of the proper size, with the natural curve are used for fan wings. The tips of two feathers, or a section may be cut from two matched feathers. All of these wings are tied on in the same manner as previously explained. See Diagram 2 for flies tied with different style wings.

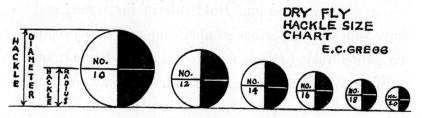

DRY FLY HACKLE SIZE CHART
E.C.GREGG

NYMPHS AND THEIR
CONSTRUCTION

NYMPHS

NYMPHS ARE LARVAE of all aquatic insects. Together with minnows, crawfish, etc., they represent about ninety per cent of the trout's regular diet. Considering this fact, it is obvious that nymphs will take trout throughout the entire season. It will greatly surprise the novice to learn of the great amount of underwater insect life present in any stream. Next time you go fishing, hold your landing net close to the bottom, in a foot or so of fast water. Reach upstream and loosen the stones and gravel. Raise your landing net, and notice the numerous nymphs that have been washed from under the stones, and have attached themselves to your net. Better still, make a screen about two feet square, from regular 14 mesh window screening. Hold this in the water, and have your fishing partner go upstream, and with a regular garden rake, or some such tool, rake up the bottom, turning over the stones and gravel. This way you can capture many nymphs. Put them in glass bottles, take them home, and make copies of them. When next you go fishing, open the first trout you catch, examine the contents of its stomach, and determine which of the copies you have made is the proper nymph or fly for the occasion. To fish with an imitation of the fly or nymph upon which they are feeding, will result in a heavier creel.

When nymph fishing, it is important to use a long, finely tapered leader. A 4x is about right. Fish in the same waters, and very much the same way as with a dry fly except that the nymph is allowed to sink. Fish upstream, or up and across the current. In the ripples. Around boulders. At the edge of fast water. Let the nymph drift with the current. Follow it with your rod tip, and be prepared to set the hook at the least hesitation of the line. Trout will sometimes take a drifting nymph and eject it, without being felt on the most delicate rod, so be ever on the alert when nymph fishing. A nymph fished down stream, and retrieved with slow, short jerks, will often work very well. When fished in this manner, trout will strike quite hard, and usually hook themselves.

There are times when trout are rolling on the surface and it seems impossible to take them on anything. It is then that they are usually feeding on nymphs, just under the surface. I remember one such time on the Housatonic River in Connecticut last summer. Just at dark, I was standing knee deep in very fast water. Trout were breaking all around me. I knew they were feeding on nymphs, and tried in every way to catch them. The water was so fast, it was impossible to keep the nymph just the right depth below the surface. I tried every trick that I knew, but could not get a strike. Finally reaching my hand in my pocket, I discovered several large buckshot. Removing the nymph from the tip of the leader, I attached five of these large shots, to the very tip of the leader, with a piece of 3x gut tippet about four inches long. I connected the nymph to the leader about sixteen inches from the tip. Within the next few minutes I took several nice trout, within rod's length of where I was standing. What actually happened, the lead was so heavy that it immediately sank straight to the bottom, and my taut line held the nymph suspended about two inches below the surface. The short gut between the nymph and the leader allowed the nymph to quiver much as the natural was doing. All the various common nymphs can be faithfully copied, by learning to tie the various styles of those herein illustrated. Simply alter the sizes, and color combinations, according to those found in the waters where you fish.

Remember nearly all the nymphs have flat bodies, and dark backs. The bodies may be flattened by thoroughly lacquering them, and when nearly dried squeezing them flat with an ordinary pair of pliers; or by

34

cutting a piece of quill the shape of the body from a turkey or goose wing. Bind this on top of the hook for the foundation of the body, and build the body over this. When finished, lacquer the entire body.

Most any body materials that are used for the making of other flies can be used; however, wool is mostly used for nymphs. Silk floss wound over a quill foundation and then lacquered, makes a very smooth, realistic body.

THEIR CONSTRUCTION
(SEE DIAGRAM 6)

Start tying silk (A) an eighth of an inch from the eye of the hook and wind closely down shank, as previously done with bucktails, wet flies, etc. Next cut a section (B) from a grey goose wing feather about one eighth inch wide, and tie on top of the hook as Fig. 1. This is to make the tail and also the back of the nymph. Bend (B) back and take a turn or two with (A) in front as Fig. 2. Tie in the ribbing (C) close to (B) Fig. 3. Next tie in body material (D) close to (C) Fig. 4. Wool yarn makes the best body material for this style nymph. Now finish the body as for a wet fly, Fig. 5, then pull (B) tightly over the top, finish off as Fig. 6. This makes a sort of hard shell over the back. Next turn the hook upside down in the vise, and lay

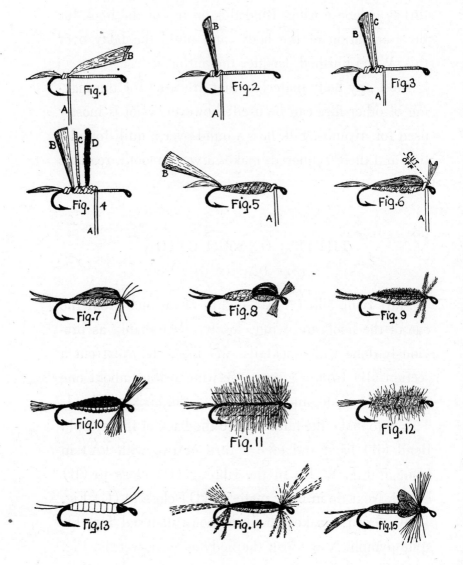

DIAGRAM 6

three horse hairs across, just in back of where the head is to be made, crisscross (A) between the hairs to spread them and make them look like legs, and your nymph should look like Fig. 7. Nymphs of this style as well as Figs. 8, 9, 10, 14 and 15 look more natural if the bodies are flattened. Fig. 8 is tied nearly the same as Fig. 7, the difference being that (C) and (D) are both wound over (B) about two-thirds of the length of the body, then (B) is turned back, the body finished as before, (B) brought forward loosely to form the humpbacked wing case, and instead of the butt end of (B) being cut off as was done with Fig. 6, it is split by crisscrossing (A) through it to form small wings as Fig. 8. Fig. 9 is made in the same way except that several strands of peacock herl is used for the dark back, tail, and feelers.

Fig. 10 is a very effective nymph, the body made entirely of natural raffia (soaked in water before using), with black hair used for the tail and feelers. The body coated with lacquer as before mentioned and pressed flat when dry; paint the back with dark brown or black lacquer.

Fig. 11 is made by close wound palmer hackle cut off on dotted lines. Fig. 12 is a fur body, made by spinning rabbit's fur or other fur on waxed tying silk and ribbing with gold; the tougher this nymph looks the more effective it seems to be. Fig. 13, the Caddis

37

worm, can be more naturally reproduced with a common rubber band than any other way I know. Get a dirty, white, rubber band about $\frac{1}{8}''$ wide, taper one end for about $\frac{1}{2}''$. Lay two horse hairs lengthwise on top of the hook for the feelers, wind tying silk over them down the hook, tie in the rubber band by the very tip of the taper, wind the tying silk back to the starting point, and be sure that the tying silk is wound smoothly. If not, any roughness will show through the rubber band. Wind the rubber band tightly to about $\frac{1}{4}''$ back of the eye. Wind back down and take one turn under the horse hairs at the tail end, wind up to the head and tie off with the tying silk. This now makes three thicknesses of the rubber band. Form a large head with the tying silk, fasten securely and you have a very realistic Caddis worm. Fig. 14 is tied about the same as Fig. 7, with a considerable amount of speckled mallard, and peacock herl, used for both the front and back feelers as well as the legs.

Fig. 15. The Damsel Nymph has a body of dark grey wool with a back of dark brown or black lacquer. Wings, small red-brown wood duck breast feathers, feelers dark brown hackle, and a large black head.

THE HELGRAMITE

(SEE DIAGRAM 7)

The Helgramite Nymph, larva of the Dobson Fly, is such an excellent bass and trout food, that the making of this nymph deserves special mention. As my personal way of making this particular nymph differs considerably from those previously explained, I consider it advisable to go into further details concerning the construction of this pattern.

I personally like the winged style. That is, with small imitation wings and horns, or feelers. This represents the nymph in its final underwater stage, just before emerging from the water as the Dobson Fly. I find black skunk tail the most satisfactory material for the body of this nymph. Either light grey swan sides, or light grey pigeon breast feathers for the wing and legs.

First wind the waxed tying silk up the shank of the hook beginning opposite the barb. Clip the fibers closely from a couple of hackle feathers. These are to form the horns. Bind these hackle quills to the top of the hook, so that the tip ends project about $1\frac{1}{2}''$ in front of the eye. Take a bunch of black skunk tail about the size of a match and bind it to the top of the hook, with tip ends towards the eye of the hook as in Diagram 7, Fig. 1. Next fold the hair forward and bind down tightly as in Fig. 2. Again fold the hair back and tie down as in

39

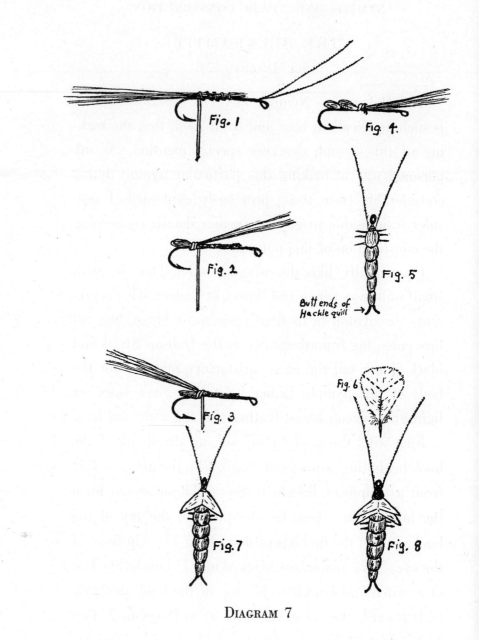

Fig. 1

Fig. 4.

Fig. 2

Fig. 5

Butt ends of
Hackle quill →

Fig. 3

Fig. 6

Fig. 7

Fig. 8

DIAGRAM 7

Fig. 3. Then again as in Fig. 4. Notice that each time the hair is folded back upon itself and tied down, that it forms a segment of the body, and that each segment increases in size, until your nymph looks like Fig. 5. At this stage turn the nymph over and tie a piece of light grey feather about $1/8''$ wide across the bottom, separate the fibers with the tying silk to form the legs. Now cut a small light grey pigeon feather with the center quill, as dotted line in Fig. 6. Give this a coat of clear lacquer: when dry, tie flat, on the back of the nymph to form the first set of wings, as in Fig. 7. Cut another feather and treat the same way, tie these slightly forward of the first set of wings, and you have a Dobson Nymph that is very lifelike in appearance.

BASS FLIES
AND FEATHER STREAMERS

IT WILL APPEAR obvious from a study of Diagram 8 (page 43) that the tying of bass flies and Feather Streamers differs so little from the tying of wet flies and bucktails that a detailed description will be unnecessary.

Bass flies are little more than large trout flies, the principal difference being the feathers that are used for the wings, although the same feathers can be used as for trout flies. It is customary with commercial tiers to use two whole feathers for the wings, or the tips of two wings feathers, etc. Place the concave sides together and tie in the butt ends the same as for a wet fly. Bass flies to be used as spinner flies, that is, flies to be used with a spinner in front, should be tied on ring eyed hooks, instead of hooks with turned down or turned up eyes.

Certain patterns of these flies have for a long time been famous as salmon flies in northern New England and Canada and the past few years have seen them steadily growing in popularity with the anglers of Connecticut, especially for Rainbow Trout. The feathers

ROYAL COACHMAN   PROFESSOR   BLACK GNAT

McGINTY   BROWN HACKLE   PARMA. BEAU

SUPERVISOR   GREGG'S DEMON

BLACK GHOST   PARMA. BELLE

Diagram 8

Bass Flies tied by the author (actual size)

that are used for wings are saddle hackles, and from four to eight feathers are used, hackles of the same size are selected, the tip ends placed even, and the concave sides of those used for the left side are placed next to the concave sides of those used for the right side, in other words, both the right and left side of the wing will be convex, or outside of the feather. Any of the standard pattern flies can be tied as streamers. Some of the patterns, however, are very elaborate flies; the Supervisor, for instance, has wings of light blue with shorter feathers of green on each side, with peacock herl along each wing, polar bear hair, jungle cock shoulders, a silver body, and a red tag. This fly was developed a few years ago by Mr. Joseph Stickney, Supervisor of Wardens, State of Maine, to imitate the smelt, a natural salmon food. The original Supervisor did not have the jungle cock or the peacock herl. Mr. Stickney suggested the addition of these feathers to me last year, and I believe that this is now the approved dressing.

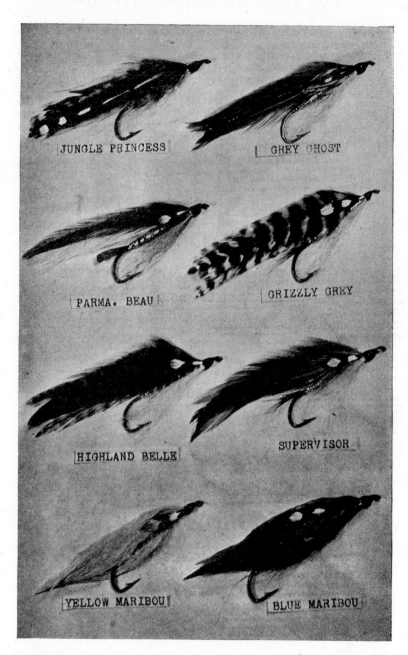

Feather Streamers tied by the author (actual size)

FAMOUS BUCKTAIL AND
FEATHER STREAMERS

SUPERVISOR: WINGS, Blue saddle hackle with polar bear hair, and peacock herl down each side. CHEEKS, green hackle tip and jungle cock. BODY, silver. TAG, red wool.

TIGER: (light) WINGS, brownish yellow bucktail or red squirrel tail. BODY, yellow chenille. TAG, gold. TAIL, barred wood duck. CHEEKS, jungle cock. THROAT, scarlet.

TIGER: (dark) WINGS, yellow bucktail. BODY, peacock herl. TAG, gold. TAIL, barred wood duck. CHEEKS, jungle cock. Short red fin.

GREGG'S DEMON: WINGS, grizzly saddle hackle dyed brown. BODY, silver ribbed with gold. CHEEKS, jungle cock. TAIL, barred wood duck. TOPPING, golden pheasant crest. HACKLE, orange.

JUNGLE PRINCESS: WINGS, grizzly saddle hackle dyed yellow with large jungle cock. CHEEKS, blue chatterer. BODY, gold tinsel. HACKLE, white.

GRIZZLY GREY: WINGS, grizzly saddle hackles. CHEEKS, jungle cock. TAIL, orange. BODY, silver tinsel. HACKLE, white bucktail.

47

HIGHLAND BELLE: WINGS, orange saddle hackles inside, grizzly saddle hackles outside. CHEEKS, jungle cock. BODY, gold tinsel ribbed with silver tinsel. HACKLE, white bucktail.

SPENCER BAY SPECIAL: WINGS, blue saddle hackles inside with furnace saddle hackles outside. CHEEKS, jungle cock. TAIL, golden pheasant tippet. BODY, silver tinsel ribbed with oval silver tinsel. HACKLE, yellow and blue mixed.

BLACK GHOST: WINGS, white saddle hackle. BODY, black silk floss ribbed with silver. CHEEKS, jungle cock. HACKLE, yellow.

GREY GHOST: WINGS, grey saddle hackle with peacock herl and white bucktail. BODY, orange floss ribbed with gold. CHEEKS, silver pheasant feather and jungle cock.

BROWN GHOST: WINGS, brown saddle hackle. BODY, brown floss ribbed with gold. CHEEKS, jungle cock. TOPPING, golden pheasant crest. TAIL, golden pheasant crest. HACKLE, yellow.

WARDEN'S WORRY: WINGS, one red and one grizzly saddle hackle. HACKLE, yellow, tied very full.

WHITE MARIBOU: WINGS, white maribou. CHEEKS, large jungle cock and small red feather. TOPPING, golden pheasant crest.

YELLOW MARIBOU: WINGS, yellow maribou. CHEEKS, large jungle cock and small red feather. TOPPING, peacock herl. Two complete maribou feathers can be used, or sections of the feathers, depending upon the size of the hook. Size 4 long shank hook is a good size to tie them for salmon.

48

FLOATING BUGS AND THEIR CONSTRUCTION

A STYLE OF FISHING becoming more popular each year is that of Fly Rod fishing with Floating Bugs. These Bugs represents the large moth, butterfly, etc., and are constructed of a large variety of materials. Some have Cork bodies. Some have Balsa Wood bodies. Others all hair bodies. Bodies covered with chenille, and other materials. One of the easiest to make, and I believe one of the most successful styles, is entirely constructed from the body hair of the deer, reindeer, or caribou. All of these hairs are rather coarse and hollow, consequently are very buoyant, and when properly made into a copy of the living insect, they have a soft, lifelike body that appears very natural when taken by a fish. These soft bodied Bugs are not so apt to be ejected before the Angler has time to set the hook, as are those with hard bodies.

Although the object of this book is to teach the Angler how to tie his own flies, a few words in regards to the writer's personal experiences in using these Bugs might not be amiss at this time. Floating Bugs are mostly tied on large size hooks, and generally used for bass. However, I have had a great deal of luck and many pleasant experiences with them tied as small as a #14 Model Perfect hook, and used with a 4x Leader. The small sizes will take many large trout, and are readily accepted by all pan fish. When fishing in still waters with the Floating Bugs, whether it be for bass, pickerel, trout or pan fish, I use a light leader, treated so that it will sink. I cast to a likely looking spot, beside an old stump, along lily pads, or to an opening in the lily pads themselves. I let the Bug hit the water with quite a splash, as a living moth of the same size would, and there I let it lie, absolutely motionless, as though stunned by the blow. By all means do not be impatient, let the Bug lie perfectly still for two or three minutes, and then simply move the tip of your rod just enough to cause the Bug to quiver on the surface. Again let it lie perfectly still for a minute or two; usually about the second time the Bug is made to quiver you can expect a strike, and when a big bass comes after one of these Bugs, he comes full of action. When fishing fast water, I fish them exactly as I would a dry fly, up-stream or up and across the current. My personal choice for color is the natural brownish grey body hair from either the deer, reindeer, or caribou. Wings, tail and body all the same natural color. I tie this pattern from size 2/0 Model perfect hook down to size 14, and use

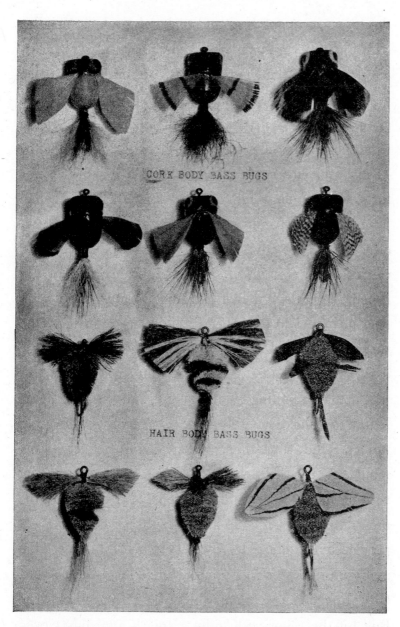

Bass Bugs tied by the author two-thirds actual size

the larger sizes for bass and pickerel, and the smaller sizes for trout and pan fish. I remember one very pleasant experience that happened in northern Maine three years ago. There is a small, deep, spring fed lake of about ten acres in area, completely surrounded by wilderness; this lake had been stocked with Rainbow Trout, and closed to all fishing for five years. I was fortunate in being there about two months after it had been opened to fishing, and was invited to try my luck, after first being advised that although some very nice catches were regularly being taken on a Streamer Fly fished deep, also on live bait and worms with a spinner, no one had ever been able to take fish on the surface. I arrived at this lake about one hour before dark, and it was one of those evenings when the water was actually boiling with rising trout. In fact never before or since have I seen so many fish breaking water at the same time. I immediately made up my mind to take fish on the surface. I began fishing with a small spider, and changed fly after fly for the next half hour with the same results as had been experienced by other dry fly fishermen. In desperation and with darkness fast approaching I tied on a size 4 Grey Bug and cast about thirty feet from shore. The Bug hit the water with quite a splash and didn't even as much as put down one fish, and several continued to rise from within a few inches to a few feet from where the Bug landed. I waited a couple of minutes and gave the Bug a little twitch, nothing happened, again I twitched and again nothing happened. I began to believe I was stumped when again the Bug was moved ever so slightly for the fifth time, and remember this was at least seven minutes after it first hit the water. A fish struck. In a few minutes I landed a 2¼ pound Rainbow. Before darkness had brought the day to a close I had landed three more beautiful Rainbows, averaging 2 pounds each. I had never since had the opportunity to fish in this beautiful little lake. Some day I hope to return, and again try, and I believe succeed in taking these beautiful Rainbow Trout on the conventional dry fly. However, this one little experience proved conclusively to me the absolute necessity of patience in fishing Floating Bugs.

FLOATING BUGS:
THEIR CONSTRUCTION

(SEE DIAGRAM 9)

First let us begin by making the most simple; that is, one that has the Body, Wings, and Tail, all of the same material and color. Follow the illustrations carefully, and even your first attempt will be a masterpiece.

Although I use well waxed 00 tying silk, you will find that regular sewing silk size A will work best on your first attempt. First wax your thread thoroughly and take a few turns around the shank of the hook and tie in a small bunch of hairs for the tail, as in Diagram 9, Fig. 1 (page 5). We will assume that we are using regular deer hair cut from the hide. Next clip a small bunch of hairs, about the size of a match, close to the hide. You will notice there is some fuzz mixed with the hair at the base close to the skin, pick out the fuzz and place the butts of the hairs under the hook as in Fig. 2. Take a couple of loose turns with the tying silk, hold the tips of the hair with the thumb and finger of the left hand, and pull the tying silk down tight. You will notice that the hairs spin around the hook and the butt ends will stand out pretty much at right angles to the hook, as in Fig. 3. Cut off the tip end of the hairs on the dotted line, press the hairs back tightly, apply a drop of water-proof lacquer to the base of the hairs and the hook, and repeat the same process of tying on a small bunch of hair, each time pressing it back tightly. Remember this is important, because the hair must be as close together as possible to make a firm, smooth, buoyant body.

When you have built the body up until it looks something like Fig. 4, remove it from the vise and with a sharp pair of scissors trim and shape it until it looks

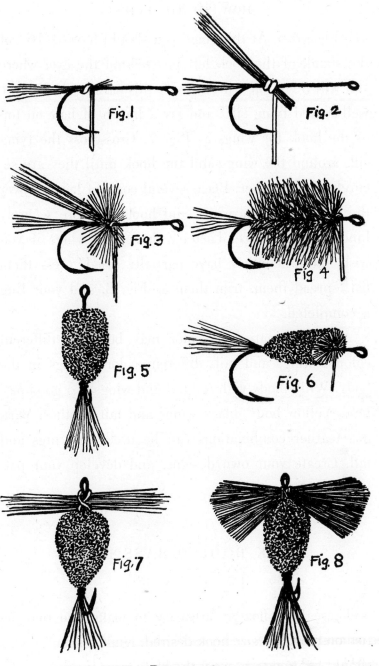

Fig. 1

Fig. 2

Fig. 3

Fig 4

Fig. 5

Fig. 6

Fig. 7

Fig. 8

DIAGRAM 9

like Figs. 5-6. At this stage you should have 3/16″ of the shank of the hook left just behind the eye, where you will tie on the wings. Cover this bare hook with the well waxed tying silk, and lay a bunch of hair on top of the hook for wings as Fig. 7. Crosscross the tying silk around the wings and the hook until they are securely tied together. Place several coats of lacquer over the junction of the wings and hook, to more securely bind them in place. Lacquer the entire wings if you wish and when they have partially dried, press them flat, spread them, trim them as Fig. 8, and your Bug is completed.

Any combination of color may be used, different colored wings and tail, different colored rings in the body. White body with red tail and wings is a good pattern. Yellow body, black wings and tail another. Various feather combinations can be used for wings and tail. Create your own designs, and develop your patterns.

CORK BODIED BASS BUGS
(SEE DIAGRAM 10)

These high floaters are easy to make and may be tied on most any size hook desired. Kinked shank hooks should be used to prevent the body from turning on the hook. Colored lacquer or enamel can be used to decorate the bodies, and eyes can be either painted on, or regular small glass eyes inserted and held in place with water-proof glue or lacquer. Any of the fancy feathers that are used for regular bass flies can be used for wings. Hair or feathers can be used for tails, etc. Let us first make one of these cork bodied Bugs on a size 1/0 hook. Take a $\frac{1}{2}''$ cork cylinder and with a razor blade shape it roughly as Diagram 10, Figs. 1-2. Then with a piece of 00 sandpaper held in the right hand and the cylinder in the left it is a very simple matter to give the body a nice smooth, shapely finish. Next cut a small V out of the body as in Fig. 3. This is easier to fit to the hook and easier to cement securely than simply making a slit in the cork. Press the V slit over the hook as in Fig. 4. Apply cement or lacquer liberally to the inside of the V slot, and to the hook shank. Press the piece that was removed securely back into place, bind tightly with string, as in Fig. 5, and let set over night. Next day when the cement has thoroughly dried and the body is permanently fastened to the hook, remove the string and with the sandpaper touch up any rough places on the body, and give a coat of lacquer or enamel of the desired color. When the body enamel has dried, take a pair of feathers for wings (whole feathers that have the quill in the centre, same as are used for regular bass fly wings are best), and with the

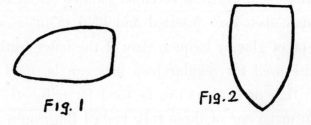

Fig. 1

Fig. 2

V. removed from Fig. 3

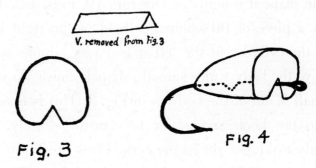

Fig. 3

Fig. 4

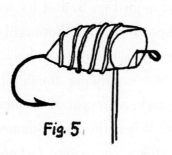

Fig. 5

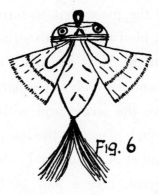

Fig. 6

DIAGRAM 10

tying silk bind these fast to the top side of the shoulders as in Fig. 6. Tie on a tail close to the body, paint on the eyes, paint any other color or designs you wish on the body, and the Bug is completed.

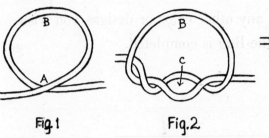
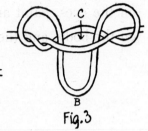

Fig.1   Fig.2   Fig.3

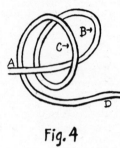
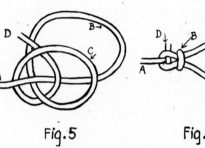

Fig.4   Fig.5   Fig.6

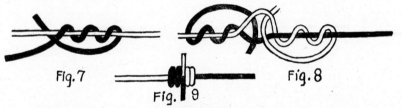

Fig.7

Fig. 9   Fig.8

Fig.10   Fig.11   Fig.12

DIAGRAM 11

ANGLERS' KNOTS

Figs. 1, 2 and 3 in Diagram 11 (page 60) show a very convenient way to tie a dropper loop in the leader; roll the gut between thumb and finger at (A) Fig. 1, next invert loop (B) through (C) Figs. 2 and 3.

Figs. 4, 5, and 6 make the best knot for a loop in the end of a leader, gut snells, etc. Pull loop (C) through loop (B) Figs. 5 and 6.

Figs. 7, 8, and 9 are about the easiest and most secure knots for making leaders, the ends are in the centre of the finished knot and can be clipped close.

Figs. 10, 11, and 12, the figure eight knot, is the best for tying flies to the leader, it won't slip, and the pull is in line with the hook shank.

MY FAVORITE FLIES

QUITE FREQUENTLY I am asked which fly I like the best, or which particular patterns I would choose should I carry only a few flies with me on a trip. That is rather a difficult question to answer. The season, the type of fishing and location must be taken into consideration.

There must be some reason for so many hundreds of patterns. I hardly believe that any half dozen patterns can be used with constant success throughout the season, even in one particular locality. There are times, when fish are feeding, that they will take anything; again one may change fly after fly without success, when finally a fly will be tried that will take fish on every cast. Suppose that particular fly wasn't included in the chosen few, the answer is obvious.

However, I will endeavor to choose six patterns each of the various styles, and to give my reasons for their choice, but here I assure you there will always be many more patterns in my fly box for further trial, after I have exhausted my favorite six.

Beginning with dry flies, my first choice would be

a Quill Gordon, on a size 16 hook. This fly closely represents the numerous duns that are on or about the water, to some extent, during the entire season. I have little faith in color in the dry fly, except light or dark shades. I do believe that the size and shape have a great deal more to do with the success of a dry fly than color. I have proven to my own satisfaction that a Quill Gordon sparsely dressed as it should be, but tied with a black hackle and yellow mallard wings, is just as successful as the customary dressing.

My second choice would be the Red Ant. Although this fly belongs to the order Hymenoptera, it can be used when many of the Diptera order are on the water, such as Cowdung, Blue Bottle, Bee, etc. This family all have flat wings and make an entirely different appearance than the aforementioned Quill Gordon. I tie the Red Ant on a size 14 hook. I build the body first of red silk floss, shape it like the body of an ant, give it a couple of coats of clear lacquer and let it dry hard and shiny. This body will reflect light, much as the natural insect. I then tie on two hackle tips for wings. Have them about as long as the hook, spread them so they are at about a 30 degree angle from the body and very flat. I then use a brown saddle hackle with fibers about 3/4" long for legs. I put on only two or three turns of the hackle, and then clip off all of the top and bottom hackles, leaving only about six fibers sticking straight out on each side. This fly will float very close to the water, and because of its sparse dressing, slightly heavy body because of the lacquer, it is not a good floater. It also has the disadvantage of being hard to see. However, it is still my second choice, and properly dressed, and fished with a very fine leader, will take many nice fish.

My third choice is the Fan Wing Royal Coachman. This fly was never supposed to represent any particular family but I believe it is taken by fish for the Lepidoptera, large-winged moths and butterflies. It seems to be very successful when these are about in the evening.

My fourth choice is the Furnace Spider. This fly I tie on a size 16 short shank hook, by winding only about three turns of a furnace saddle hackle, with fibers about three fourths of an inch long. Tied in this manner, without any body or tail, the fly will alight on the water with the hook down, and looked at from beneath, against the light, only the little round black spot will be noticeable. This I believe represents some of the order Coleoptera (beetles) and also the small black gnat (Empidae). I know of no other ways to tie the Black Gnat small enough to represent the natural insect, and even on the very smallest hook, the artificial is usually many times larger than the natural. The small black centre of the furnace saddle hackle tied in this manner seems to represent the size of the natural very closely. This fly is a very good floater, and an excellent fly when trout are feeding on those small insects.

My fifth choice is the Grannon. This fly is of the order of Trichoptera, and has different shaped wings than any of those previously mentioned, the wings being quite full and roof shaped. It is on the water a good part of the season, and can be used when other flies with this shape wing are about, such as the alder fly, cinnamon fly, etc.

My next and sixth choice of dry fly would be the Brown Palmer, made on a size 12 long shank hook with a full body of peacock herl, and palmer hackle, wound not too full. This I believe is taken by the trout for many of the caterpillars.

My personal choice of these six patterns should now appear quite obvious, should it be necessary for me to limit myself to such a small selection. I have selected one each of the six most prominent orders, and should any one of the hundreds of families of these orders be in prominence on the water, I would at least have the correct size or color.

My choice of the standard pattern wet flies, Feather Streamers, Bucktail Streamers, and nymphs would be a little more difficult. I am a firm believer that color plays a very important part in the dressing of wet flies, as well as size and style. I offer my personal choice of these styles because of the consistency with which they have taken fish for me during many years of fishing all parts of the country.

I do not hesitate to say that I have taken more trout, of all kinds, on a brown hackle with peacock herl body, than any of the other common wet fly patterns. This is probably because I have used it more. I do believe that in the north, and especially for brook trout, a fly with a little red in it is more productive. Therefore, for northern fishing I would select Royal Coachman, Parmachene Belle, and Montreal. Other favorite flies that are good most anywhere in North America are Grizzly King, Queen O'Waters; Cahill, and Grey Hackle.

Feather Streamers and Hair Streamers are being more extensively used each year. Many authorities are of firm conviction that these flies unquestionably represent small minnows, upon which the fish are in the habit of feeding. This may be true, but I have seen many rubber, metal and composition minnows, that were exact replicas of the naturals, both as to color and size, and they would not take fish as would the Feather or Hair Streamers, fished in the same waters, at the same time.

Most of my experience with Feather Streamers and also Hair Streamers has been for Landlocked Salmon and Rainbow Trout, in big waters. So I will list these according to the way they have produced for me. The

Black Ghost on a #4 long shank hook has been my most successful Feather Streamer. Probably because its white streamers are easily seen by the fish. It will most always raise fish, even if not the proper fly to make them strike. The Grey Ghost is another, and one of the most popular streamers in the North for Land-locked Salmon. This fly, as well as the Supervisor, Spencer Bay Special and numerous other flies of this style, were originally designed by their creators to represent the smelt, a favorite food of the salmon. These flies vary so in their color combinations that I wonder what the fish do take them for. However, I do know that a Grey Ghost will work when a Supervisor will not, and vice versa. One is grey and the other is blue. When fishing in lakes with a Feather Streamer for trout I have consistently had most luck with a creation of my own, Gregg's Demon. This fly was never tied to represent anything, but I have taken many nice fish on it, and have seen little fellows hardly as long as the fly itself chase it, and try their best to bite it in two. There is just something about it that has "fish appeal."

A Brown Bucktail with a silver body on a #6 3x long shank hook, rates number one in Bucktail Streamers. Another excellent fly that has been a favorite for years, is a Yellow and Red Bucktail, with a silver body, the red only a narrow streak through the centre. This fly has recently been named "Mickey Finn." A red and white, with silver or gold body, is a real good pattern where there are brook trout, and tied on a large hook is very good for bass.

I use one with all white bucktail and silver body, the same as I do a Black Ghost, for locating fish. I find they will most always show their presence, one way or another, when a white fly is cast near them.

An all yellow with black streak in the centre same as the "Mickey Finn" is another very good combination. This is an excellent pickerel and bass fly. In fact, most any of these Feather Streamers and Bucktail Streamers, tied on larger hooks, and used with or without a spinner, are excellent lures for both bass and pickerel.

Nymphs: I have explained elsewhere my liking for these lures, and can say little more, except that I always carry the following color combinations in various sizes. All tied according to styles illustrated in the diagrams. Cream Belly with Dark Back; Yellow Belly with Black Ribs and Dark Back; Green Belly with Dark Back; Grey Belly and Gold Ribs with Dark Back; Brown Belly and Gold Ribs with Black Back; Orange Belly and Black Ribs with Dark Back.

STANDARD DRESSINGS OF 334 FLIES

ALPHABETICALLY ARRANGED

NAME	TAG	TAIL	RIBS	BODY	HACKLE	WINGS
Abbey		Orange & black	Gold	Red Floss	Brown	Grey Mottled (mallard)
Adams	Gold	Golden tippet		Grey Wool	Brown and grizzly	Grey Mottled (mallard)
Alexandra		Peacock herl		Silver	Black	Peacock sword and jungle cock
Alder				Peacock herl	Black	Dark speckled Turkey or Grouse
Apple Green		Brown		Green Silk	Brown	Dark Grey
Ash Dun		Grey		Silver Grey	Grey	Lt. Starting
August Dun		Reddish	Yellow	Lt. Brown floss	Reddish Br.	Hen Pheasant
Autumn Dun		Black	Yellow	Black	Grey	Teal Breast
Babcock		Black & yellow	Gold	Cardinal Red	Black	Black & Yellow
Barrington		Grey Speckled		Peacock Herl	Brown	Grey Speckled
Beauty				Black	Badger	Spotted golden
Beaverkill	Gold	Grey Speckled	Silver	White floss	Brown tied palmer	Grey
Bee	Gold			Black & Yellow chenille	Brown	Brown
Belgrade	Peacock herl	Scarlet and white		Yellow	Claret tied palmer	Red, white and jungle cock
Blue Rooster		Tan mottled wood duck		Condor Quill	Blue	Tan mottled wood duck
Blue Bi-visible					Andalusian	
Black Bi-visible				Blue floss	Blue, tied palmer	
Blue Winged olive		Brown		Black floss	Black, tied palmer	Blue dun hackle tips
				Green	Golden Brown	

69

NAME	TAG	TAIL	RIBS	BODY	HACKLE	WINGS
Blue Professor	Gold	Scarlet	Gold	Blue floss	Ginger	Grey speckled
Black Nymph		Brown mottled	Gold	Black Herl	Partridge	
Brown Nymph		Brown mottled		Brown Herl	Partridge	
Br. Bi:Visible			Silver or none	Brown	Brown	
Brown Spider				Brown	Brown	
Black Spider				Black	Black	
Brown Dun		Brown		Brown	Brown	Starling
Black Midge				Black	Black	
Black Prince	Silver	Scarlet	Silver	Black floss	Black	Black
Blue Dun		Pale blue hackle		Pale blue fur	Pale blue dun	Blue Grey
Blue Bottle	White Silk		Black or Gold	Steel blue silk or dk. blue chenille	Black or grey	Black or grey
Black Gnat	Gold			Black Chenille	Black	Grey
Black Hackle	Gold			Black Chenille	Black	
Blue Upright		Pale blue hackle		Pale Blue Fur	Pale blue dun	Blue Grey
Brown Hackle	Gold	Golden tippet		Peacock Herl	Brown	
Brown Palmer	Gold	Golden tippet		Peacock Herl	Brown tied palmer	
Brown Hen	Red Silk			Peacock Herl	Brown	Brown mottled
Blue Quill		Blue dun hackle		Quill	Blue Dun	Blue Grey
Black and Silver		Golden tippet		Silver	Black	Black
Black and Claret		Golden tippet	Silver	Claret Wool	Black	Black
Black June			Silver	Peacock Herl	Black	Dark Grey
Black Moose		Green and Yellow		Green Quill	Black, tied palmer	Guinea
Black Quill				Quill	Black	Dark Grey
Black Ant	Black chenille	Black		Black Silk	Black	Slate

Name		Tail		Body	Hackle	Wing
Blue and Black		Golden tippet	Gold	Black	Black	Blue Jay
Blue Jay	Gold	Scarlet		Red	Red	Grey
Blue Quill		Blue Dun	Gold	Quill	Blue Dun	Grey
Bonnie View	Gold	Grey	Gold	Olive Brown	Brown	Black
Boots Black	Gold	Speckled	Gold	Red Wool	Black	Grey Speckled
Brandreth	Gold	Scarlet	Red	Yellow	Scarlet and yellow	Black and brown mottled
Brown Adder	Red	Black & Br. mottled		Brown Silk	Brown, tied palmer	Brown
Brown Sedge	Gold		Gold	Brown Silk	Brown	
Bustard and Black	Silver	Golden tippet	Silver	Black Wool	Black	
Bustard and Orange	Gold	Golden tippet	Gold	Orange Wool	Orange	
Butcher		Scarlet	Gold	Silver	Black	Blue black
Caddis	Gold	Grey	Gold	Brown Silk	Brownish Red	Grey
Cahill, Dark	Gold	Tan Mottled		Grey Wool or Fur	Brown	Tan mottled wood duck
Cahill, Light	Gold	Tan Mottled		Buff Wool	Ginger	Tan Mottled
Cahill Quill		Tan Mottled		Quill	Grey	Tan Mottled
Canada	Gold	Claret	Gold	Bright Red	Brown	Mottled Turkey
Caperer	Gold			Rusty red wool	Red	Hen Pheasant
Cardinal		Red	Gold	Red Wool	Light red	Red
Claret Gnat	Gold		Gold	Claret Wool	Claret	Dark Grey
Cinnamon		Golden tippet	Gold	Lemon & Black Wool	Brown	Cinnamon
Coachman	Gold	Golden tippet		Peacock Herl	Brown	White
Coachman Leadwing	Gold	Golden tippet		Peacock Herl	Brown	Dark Grey
Cock-y-bondhu	Gold		Gold	Peacock Herl	Furnace	
Col. Fuller		Black and yellow	Yellow silk	Scarlet	Yellow	Yellow and scarlet

NAME	TAG	TAIL	RIBS	BODY	HACKLE	WINGS
Cow Dung				Dirty orange herl or yel. green wool	Brown	Grey
Critchley Fancy	Gold	Yellow	Gold	Yellow	Yellow and grey	Grizzly and scarlet
Cupsuptic		Golden tippet	Silver	Red Silk Floss	Brown	Yellow
Dark Sedge			Gold Wire	Dk. Green Wool	Blood Red	
Dark Stone			Yellow Silk	Grey Wool	Grey	Dark grey
Dr. Breck		Grey Speckled		Silver	Scarlet	White and Scarlet
Dorset		Furnace		Green Wool	Furnace	Teal
Downlooker		Furnace		Brown Floss	Brown, tied palmer	Brown and black mottled turkey
Deer Fly		Black		Bright Green	White	White
Dusty Miller		Grey speckled	Gold Wire	Grey wool or mohair	Grey	Dirty Grey Turkey
Dark Butcher	Gold	Br. Hackle	Brown Silk	Scarlet		Yellow and black
Emerald				Lt. Green	Lt. Brown	Brown Mottled
Evening Dun		Lt. Blue	Gold	Buff Wool	Lt. Blue	Starling
Epting		Grey speckled		Red, orange, & yel. chenille	Black	Grey Speckled
Female Beaverkill	Yellow chenille	Grey speckled		Grey silk or wool	Brown	Dark Grey
Female Grannon	Green			Brown Floss	Partridge	Brown mottled partridge
Fem. March Br.			Yellow Silk	Dk. brown floss	Partridge	Brown mottled turkey or grouse
Ferguson	Scarlet yel. and herl		Silver	Yellow Floss	Lt. Green	Mottled turkey tail, yellow and red
Fern Fly				Orange Floss	Lt. Red	Dark Starling
Feted Green		Green		Green	Green	Green

72

					R. I. Red	Bronze
Fiery Brown	Gold	Golden tippet	Gold	Reddish brown mohair or wool		
Flights Fancy		Ginger	Gold	Pale Yel. Floss	Ginger	Lt. Grey
Francis Fly			Red Silk	Peacock Herl		Grizzly Dun
Furnace Dun	Gold	Furnace		Br. & orange wool	Furnace	Dark Starling
Furnace Hackle				Peacock Herl	Furnace	
Gen. Hooker	Brown hairs	Gold	Yellow	Green Floss	Brown	Mottled grey and brown
Great Dun			Gold	Brown Floss	Brown	Dark Grey
Grey Bi-Visible			Silver or none		Grizzly	
Green Nymph		Green	Gold	Green Wool	Green	
Grey Spider				Grey	Grizzly	
Gld. Midge			Gold	Pale Green	Dun	
Great Dun	Gold	Brown Hairs	Gold	Brown Silk	Brown	Dark Grey
Ginger Palmer	Silver		Silver	Yellow or ginger floss	Ginger, tied palmer	
Ginger Quill	Gold	Ginger		Quill	Ginger	Lt. Grey
Golden Dun	Gold	Grey Speckled	Gold	Gold or orange	Red	Lt. Grey
Golden Dun Midge		Grey Speckled		Pale Green Wool	Light Grey	Dark Grey
Gold Spinner	Gold	Grey Hairs	Gold	Gold	Red	Lt. Grey
Gold Eyed Gauze Wing		Blue Dun		Pale yel. and green silk	Blue Dun	Blue dun hackle tips
Gold Monkey				Yellow Silk Floss	Grey Speckled	Dark Grey
Gold Ribbed Hare's Ear	Gold	Dark Hairs	Gold	Rabbit's Fur		Grey

NAME	TAG	TAIL	RIBS	BODY	HACKLE	WINGS
Gold Stork		Grey speckled		Gold	Brown	Grey speckled
Golden Eyed Gauze Wing				Pale Grey	Pale Grey	Pale Green
Good Evening	Gold	Orange	Gold	Scarlet	Brown	Dark blue with white tip
Gordon	Gold	Brown speckled	Gold	Yellow	Grey	Brown speckled wood duck
Governor		Scarlet		Peacock Herl	Brown	Brown mottled turkey
Gov. Alford				Green Herl	Brown	Black and Brown
Grannon				Brown fur or wool	Brown or grizzly	Dark Partridge
Gravelbed	Gold			Dark Grey	Black	Woodcock
Grey Drake		Grey Speckled	Black	White Floss	Grey	Grey speckled
Grey Hackle peacock	Gold	Golden tippet		Peacock Herl	Grizzly	
Grey Hackle		Golden tippet		Red wool or silk	Grizzly	
Grey Hackle yellow	Gold	Golden tippet		Yellow Wool or Silk	Grizzly	
Grey Marlow	Gold		Gold	Red Wool	Grey	Grey
Grey Miller				Grey Wool	Grey	Grey
Great Dun		Brown and Grey		Maroon	Grey or Black	Grey or Black
Great Red spinner		Black and white	Gold	Purple and Red Floss	Brown	Slate Grey
Grey Bodied Ashy		Golden tippet		Brown, black, or green herl or wool	Grey	
Green Drake		Brown pheasant	Brown Floss	Raffia or lemon silk	Partridge & ginger	Yellowish Olive
Green Insect				Green Herl	Cream	

Lake Edward		Golden crest	Gold	Claret Wool	Claret	Pea Green
Lake George		White and scarlet	Gold	Scarlet floss	White	White & Scarlet
Lake Green			Green Silk	Canary yellow	Ginger	Teal Breast
Laramie		Scarlet	Silver	Scarlet floss	Dark Blue	Grey Mottled
Lt. Stone		Grey	Yellow Silk	Grey	Grey	Grey
Little Marryat		Brown		Lt. grey or herl	Brown	Dark grey
Ld. Baltimore			Black Silk	Orange Silk	Black	Black and jungle
Lowery				Peacock Herl	Brown	Lt. Brown
Lt. Montreal	Gold	Grey Mottled	Gold	Scarlet	Claret	Grey Speckled
Lt. March Br.		Partridge hackle		Olive & Br. fur	Partridge	Lt. mottled partridge
Magpie		Black Hairs		Black	Black	Black with white tip
Mallard & Amber	Gold	Golden tippet	Gold	Amber floss	Lt. Red	Brown mallard breast
Mallard & Claret	Gold	Golden tippet	Gold	Claret wool	Lt. Red	Brown mallard breast
Mallard & Green	Gold	Golden tippet	Gold	Green Wool	Lt. Red	Brown mallard breast
Mallard & Red	Gold	Golden tippet	Gold	Red wool	Lt. Red	Brown mallard breast
March Brown		Grouse	Yellow Silk	Br. or Grey fur	Grouse	Dark Brown mottled turkey or grouse
March Br. Ginger		Ginger		Brown fur	Ginger	Dark Brown mottled turkey or grouse
March Br. Nymph		Partridge	Gold	Yellow wool	Partridge	Dark Brown with white tips
Markham		Scarlet and white		Yellow	Scarlet	
Marlow Buzz			Gold	Peacock Herl	Furnace	Dark Grey
Marston's Fancy				Brown Fur	Brown	Canary yellow
Massasaga	Gold	Ibis	Gold	Green floss	Canary Yellow	
Maxwell Blue		Lt. Blue	Silver	Grey	Lt. Blue	
McGinty		Grey speckled and scarlet		Black and yel. chenille	Brown	Brown with white tip

NAME	TAG	TAIL	RIBS	BODY	HACKLE	WINGS
Mealy Moth				Lt. Grey Wool	White	White
Mershon	Silver	Black Hairs	Silver	Black	Black	Dark blue with white tip
Merson White		Black Hairs	Silver	White	Black	Dark blue
Mole	Gold	Brown Hairs	Gold	Dk. brown floss	Brown tied palmer	Brown mottled mallard
Montreal		Scarlet	Gold	Claret floss	Claret	Brown mottled turkey tail or grouse
Montreal Claret	Gold	Claret	Gold	Claret floss	Claret	Brown mottled turkey tail or grouse
Montreal Silver		Scarlet		Silver	Claret	Brown mottled turkey tail or grouse
Montreal Yellow	Gold	Scarlet	Gold	Yellow floss	Claret	Brown mottled turkey tail or grouse
Morrison		Black	Black	Claret	Black	Black
Mowry		Black Hairs		Black	Black	Black with white tip
Needle Brown				Orange	Dark Brown	
Neversink		Black		Pale buff wool	Yellow	Teal breast
New Page	Gold	Gold	speckled	Yellow floss	Brown	Mottled brown and red
Olive Dun	Gold	Olive Dun	Gold or none	Olive Wool	Olive Dun	Lt. blue grey or olive dun tackle tips
Olive Quill		Olive		Quill	Olive	Olive
Orange & Bk.	Gold	Golden tippet	Gold	Orange Wool	Black	
Orange Dun				Orange Wool	Dk. Brown	Lt. Brown
Olive Nymph		Olive		Mot. Br. wool	Olive	
Orange Miller			Gold	Orange floss	White	White
Orange Sedge			Gold	Orange floss	Brown tied palmer	Red, Brown
Oriole		Yellow	Gold	Black floss	Black	Yellow

78

Fly	Tag	Tail	Rib	Body	Hackle	Wing
Oak		Black		Orange floss	Brown	Dark grey and Lt. Brown mottled
Pale Blue Dun		Pale Blue		Pale Blue Fur	Pale Blue	Pale blue hackle tips or none
Pale Buff		Pale Buff	Br. silk or none	Pale Buff Wool	Pale Buff	Pale Buff
Pale Eve. Dun				Lemon floss	Lt. blue grey or grizzly	Lt. Blue Grey
Pale Sulphur		Pale Yel. Hairs		Pale Yellow	Pale Yellow	Pale Yellow
Orange Tag						
Pale Watery		Yellow		Olive Wool	Pale Yellow	Grey
Pale Watery Quill		Yellow		Quill	Pale Yellow	Grey
Pale Yellow				Yellow	Yellow	Pale Yellow
Parmachene Beau	Peacock herl	Scarlet and white	Gold	Yellow floss or mohair	Scarlet and white	Scarlet, White jungle cock
Parmachene Belle	Peacock herl	Scarlet and white	Gold	Yellow floss or mohair	Scarlet and White	Scarlet & white
Parson		Golden tippet	Silver wire	Silver	Black	Bronze
Peter Ross		Golden tippet		Bright Yel.	Ginger	
Pheasant			Gold	Yellow floss	Ginger	Bronze
Pheasant, Gold		Golden tippet	Gold Wire	Gold	Pheasant	Pheasant, Wing
Pheasant, Silver		Golden tippet	Silver wire	Silver	Pheasant	Pheasant, Wing
Pheasant & Yel.		Golden tippet	Gold	Yellow floss	Pheasant	Pheasant, Wing
Pink Lady	Gold	Pheasant	Gold	Pink floss	Brown	Grey Speckled
Pink Wickhams		Brown		Pink floss	Brown tied palmer	Grey Speckled
Polka	Gold	Scarlet	Gold	Scarlet floss	Scarlet	Guinea
Poor Mans Fly		Ginger		Brown Wool	Ginger	Grey Speckled

NAME	TAG	TAIL	RIBS	BODY	HACKLE	WINGS
Portland		Grey Speckled	Gold	Red floss	Red	Teal Breast
Preston's Fancy		Brown Hairs		Gold	Brown	Grey with white spot
Priest		Red Ibis	Silver	Silver	Badger	
Prime Gnat				Brown	Brown	Dark Grey
Professor	Gold	Scarlet	Gold	Yellow floss	Brown	Grey Speckled
Quaker			Silver	Grey Wool	Grey	Grey Speckled
Queen O'Waters			Gold	Orange floss	Br. Palmer	Grey Speckled
Quill Gordon		Tan speckled	Gold Wire or none	Quill	Blue Dun	Tan speckled wood duck
Raven		Golden tippet		Black chenille	Black	Black Crow
Red Ant	Herl			Red floss	Brown	Dark Grey
Red Fox		Speckled Teal		Reddish Brown	Red. Brown	Teal
Red Quill		Dark Red		Red Quill	Dark Red	Med. Starling
Red Ibis		Scarlet	Gold	Scarlet floss	Scarlet	Scarlet
Red Spinner	Gold	Brown Hairs	Gold	Red	Brown	Dark Grey
Red Tag	Red Silk	Red		Peacock Herl	Brown	
Rd. Bod. Ashy				Red Wool	Brown Palmer	
Ross McKenney	Gold	Barred wood duck	Gold	Brown Wool		White and red bucktail and jungle cock
Royal Coachman	Gold	Golden tippet		Peacock herl with scarlet red band	Hackle Brown	White
Rube Wood	Red	Grey Speckled		White Chenille	Lt. Brown	Grey Speckled
Ruben Wood		Tan speckled		White Chenille	Lt. Brown	Tan speckled
Saltoun		Ginger	Silver	Black floss	Black	Lt. Starling
Sand-Fly		Lt. Ginger		Copper Brown	Lt. Ginger	Yellowish Brown
Sassy Cat		Scarlet		Peacock Herl	Yellow	Yellow, scarlet cheeks

Seth Green Claret			Yellow	Green floss	Claret	Grey speckled
Seth Green Turkey			Yellow	Green floss	Brown	Brown mottled
Shad Fly			Green	Peacock Herl	Brown	Brown mottled
Shoemaker		Tan speckled		Pink & Grey		Mottled Woodcock
Silver Doctor		Yel. blue green and red		Silver	Blue & Guinea	Brown, red, blue, green and yellow
Silver Horns				Copper floss	Grouse	Brown
Silver Sedge				Silver	Brown Palmer	Teal breast
Silver Stock		Grey Speckled		Silver	Brown	
Soldier Palmer		Brown	Gold	Red Wool	Brown Palmer	
Spent Gnat			Peacock herl	Wt. Floss or Quill	Ginger	Blue Hkl. tips
Sedge, light				Pale Buff wool	Snipe	Hen pheasant
Sniper & Yel.				Pale Yel. floss	Grouse	
Stebbins		Grey Speckled		Peacock Herl		Dark Starling
Stone		Grey	Yellow	Grey Wool	Grey	Grey
Sunset	Green chenille			Yellow chenille	Yellow	White
Swiftwater		Grey Speckled	·	Peacock herl, Orange floss band	Brown	White
Teal & Black	Gold	Golden tippet		Black wool	Black	Teal breast
Teal & Orange		Golden tippet	Gold	Orange wool	Olive	Teal breast
Teal & Gold	Gold	Golden tippet		Gold	Dk. Brown	Teal breast
Teal & Red		Golden tippet	Gold	Red wool	Olive	Teal breast
Teal & Silver	Silver	Golden tippet		Silver	Badger	Teal breast
Teal & Yellow		Golden tippet	Silver	Yellow wool	Ginger	Teal breast

NAME	TAG	TAIL	RIBS	BODY	HACKLE	WINGS
Tippet & Black	Silver	Golden tippet	Silver	Black wool	Black	Golden Tippet
Tippet & Red	Silver	Golden tippet	Silver	Red wool	Dk. Brown	Golden Tippet
Tippet & Silver	Silver	Golden tippet	Silver	Silver	Badger	Golden Tippet
Tootle Bug	Blue	Scarlet		Orange & Yel.	Br. palmer	Brown Mottled
Tups Indispensable		Honey Dun		Yellow	Honey Dun	
Turkey Brown			Red	Brown	Brown	Brown
Turkey Professor	Gold	Red		Yellow floss	Brown	Brown mottled
Van Patten		Scarlet	Gold	White	Brown	Grey Speckled
Variant, Gold				Gold	Blue Dun	Starling
Water Cricket			Black	Orange	Black	
Watson's Fancy	Gold	Golden tippet	Gold	Red & Blk. wool	Black	Black hackle tips
Welshman's Button				Peacock Herl	Furnace	Landrail
Western Bee				Yellow & Black chenille	Brown	Dark Grey
Whirling Blue Dun	Gold	Ginger		Blue Grey Fur	Ginger	Blue Grey
White Hackle			Silver	White floss	White	White
White Miller			Silver	White floss	White	White
White Moth	Silver			White Chenille	White	
Wickham's Fancy		Brown hairs		Gold	Br. palmer	Grey
Wickham Pink		Red		Red & Gold	Lt. Reddish	Landrail
Widow			White	Purple Floss	Black	Black
Willow			Yellow	Green	Brown	Dark Grey
Wilson				Orange	Orange	Teal breast
Witch Gold	Gold	Red Ibis	Gold	Grey Wool	Badger	Lt. Grey
Whitchurch Dun		Grey Speckled		Yellow floss	Ginger	
White Wickhams		Brown Hairs		White floss	White, palmer	Grey

Woodcock & Gold		Golden tippet	Silver	Gold	Ginger	Mottled Woodcock
Woodcock & Grn.		Golden tippet	Silver	Green wool	Green	Mottled Woodcock
Woodcock & Red		Golden tippet	Silver	Red wool	Reddish brown	Mottled Woodcock
Woodcock & Yel.		Golden tippet	Silver	Yellow wool	Woodcock	Mottled Woodcock
Worm Fly				Peacock Herl	Ginger	
Yel. Bi-visible				Yellow Wool	Yel. and white palmer	
Yel. Coachman				Peacock herl	Brown	Yellow
Yel. Dun				Yellow wool	Honey Dun	Lt. Starling
Yel. Hackle			Gold	Yellow floss	Yellow	
Yel. Professor	**Gold**	Scarlet	Gold	Yellow floss	Brown	Yellow Speckled
Yel. May		Yellow Speckled	Gold or black	Yellow floss	Yellow	Yellow Speckled
Yel. Miller			Gold	Yel. & Herl	White	White
Yel. Spider		Yellow		Yellow	Yel. (long)	White
Yel. Sally		Yellow	Gold	Yellow	Yellow	
Zulu	**Gold**	Red		Peacock Herl	Black	Yellow